Single But Not Alone
Prayers of a Single Parent

Kimberly Jo Holmes

SINGLE BUT NOT ALONE: PRAYERS OF A SINGLE PARENT

Published by CreateSpace, a DBA of On-Demand Publishing LLC, part of the Amazon group of companies.

Unless otherwise indicated, Scripture quotations in this book are taken from the Holy Bible, New International Version ®. Copyright © 1973, 1978, 1984 by the International Bible Society. Used by permission of Zondervan Publishing House. The "NIV" and "New International Version" trademarks are registered in the United States Patent and Trademark Office by International Bible Society.

The definitions were in part taken from Dictionary.com, Copyright ©2014 Dictionary.com, LLC. All rights reserved, and in part by the heart and opinion of the author.

ISBN-13: 978-1497360396

Copyright © 2014 by Kimberly Holmes

The stories in this book are true, but many names have been changed to protect the privacy of the persons involved.

All rights reserved. No part of this work may be reproduced, transmitted, stored or used in any form or by any means graphic, electronic, or mechanical, including but not limited to photocopying, recording, scanning, digitizing, taping, Web distribution, information networks or information storage and retrieval systems, or in any manner whatsoever without prior written permission. For further information, contact Kimberly Holmes at kimholmes04@gmail.com.

Printed in the United States of America

Acknowledgments

With special thanks to:

First and foremost, to my heavenly Father, for entrusting me with my precious children in the first place, for giving me what I didn't deserve – His amazing grace, for His forgiveness, for His unstoppable love for me, for His pursuit of me, for His loving patience while He waited for me to finish what He asked of me, and for His beautiful presence, of which I am nothing without.

To my daughter, Kristin, and my son, Jason, for being my inspiration to be a better person and a better parent, for giving me permission to write from my heart and share our stories, and for supporting me and encouraging me to write this book.

To my new sweet husband, Randy, for his unwavering love, support, and belief in this book and the calling that God has given to me.

To my extraordinary editor, Tim Grissom, for believing in me and for his extremely invaluable insight and sensitivity to others' needs as he challenged me to dig a little deeper to relay a message.

To my grammar editor, Fran Taylor, for her valuable input and trained skills to bring polish to my words.

To my amazing sisters and best friends, Jeri and Cindy, for believing in me and encouraging me to stay strong and true to myself.

To my friend, Pastor Chris Bunkoff, who prodded me (and constantly nagged me) to complete my manuscript, because he believed in the importance of this message.

Finally, to my mom and dad, Bob and Shirley, for giving me such an incredible example to trust in the Lord, to pray without ceasing, and to love unconditionally.

I love you all.

Endorsements

"This book is an incredibly thoughtful and practical encouragement to pray for our children. Although it is written specifically with the single parent in mind, even parents in solid marriages will do well to apply the prayer principles this material covers. The prayer examples are born out of personal experience and followed up with Scriptures to root and ground our prayers in God's Word. This is not a book to just be read. This is a handbook to write in and use as a personal prayer guide to lift our children up to God's throne of grace and mercy to find needed grace and help for our children."
Patrick M. Brown – Pastor, Northlake Baptist Church, Dallas, Texas

"It's not every day that you find a book that speaks directly to your heart and the emotions that you're managing during a relationship crisis. *Single But Not Alone* is that book. Whether male or female, the hurts, the tears, the pain, and fears that you're facing are real and can seem overwhelming. Regardless of when your separation or divorce took place, the words inside ring loud and clear. *Single But Not Alone* is a journey through pain, the discovery of hope, and a guide that points you toward a peace that can only come from God. I pray it blesses you as it has me."
Pastor Chris Bunkoff – Executive Director, Single Parent Advocate, Dallas, Texas

Those who hope in the LORD
will renew their strength.
They will soar on wings like eagles;
they will run and not grow weary,
they will walk and not be faint.
—Isaiah 40:31

CONTENTS

Preface

Praying for Yourself

1. Forgive Me, Lord
2. Help Me to Forgive
3. Renew My Heart
4. Give Me Peace
5. Humble Me
6. Remove the Loneliness
7. Give Me Wisdom
8. Bridle My Tongue
9. Show Me How to Serve

Praying for Your Children

10. Heal Their Broken Hearts
11. Give Them Peace
12. Renew Their Hearts with Joy
13. Fill Their Emptiness
14. Take Away Their Feelings of Guilt
15. Teach Them to Forgive
16. Show Them Healthy Boundaries
17. Help Them Let Go of the Past
18. Give Them a Desire to Honor Their Parents
19. Teach Them Humility
20. Show Them Your Plan

Conclusion

Preface

The love of parents for their children is profound. There is an immeasurable force behind it. If you need proof, try taking a newborn from her mother or bullying a little boy in his father's presence. Yet, as strong as this love is, it does not compare to the love God has for His children. He is a Father to the fatherless and a provider to the disadvantaged.

Single But Not Alone was born during a difficult time in my life. My children were needy and fatherless. They had a natural father but he lived hours away and did not have much contact, which caused deep hurt in their hearts that I could not fix. All I knew to do was pray.

As I cried out to God during my darkest moments, I found out who my Abba Father was. The Scripture says in Romans 8:14–16: "Those who are led by the Spirit of God are sons of God. For you did not receive a spirit that makes you a slave again to fear, but you received the Spirit of sonship. And by him we cry, 'Abba, Father.' The Spirit himself testifies with our spirit that we are God's children."

Praise God that we can be called His children. As I rested in this truth, I received it for my children as well. I cleared my mind and positioned my heart before His throne, and through that I learned that though I was single, I was not alone.

PART ONE

Praying for Yourself

As parents, not only do we have an obligation to demonstrate godliness to our children, we also have an opportunity to exemplify God's love for them. If we can communicate to our children the love of God, we have imparted a very good thing, and possibly their first steps toward healing. To do this we ourselves must be willing to evaluate our own condition.

When we take an inventory of our heart, we also take a step toward pursuing healthy relationships, especially with those who are closest to us. The Bible says in Mark 11:25–26 that in order for our heavenly Father to forgive us, we need to repent from our transgressions. With unforgiveness, bitterness, discontentment, pride, or any variety of sins lurking in our soul, our relationships both with God and with others are hindered.

But we have an opportunity to change that.

These next nine short chapters were written for you, the parent. Use this time to examine your own heart and acknowledge any changes that may need to take place inside of you. Be willing to forgive, to let go of the past, and to change your thinking, so as to reposition yourself to become a better *you*. I challenge you to purposefully demonstrate the character you wish to see in your children. They are watching you react and, whether they admit it or not, they're looking for an example to follow. Is your heart ready to lead?

> Therefore confess your sins to each other and pray for
> each other so that you
> may be healed. The prayer of a righteous man is
> powerful and effective.
> —James 5:16

1

Forgive Me, Lord

> In Him we have redemption through his blood, the
> forgiveness of sins, in accordance with the riches of
> God's grace that he lavished on us with all
> wisdom and understanding.
> —Ephesians 1:7–8

Forgive: to stop feeling anger toward someone; to set free, as if the Lord forgave you and set you free

We all need to be forgiven, don't we? Yet we walk around every day thinking we can't ask for forgiveness, believing our choices were just too much for God to forgive *again*. Our shame convinces us that God has set a limit on how many times He will put up with our failures. But He has not!

I felt so much shame from my divorce and from falling short in my marriage. My perspective of God was clouded, and I felt unworthy of forgiveness. I have struggled with this many times, over issues both big and small. When I've realized that I have disappointed others, and myself, I have often wondered if I could even ask again, "Lord, will You forgive me?"

When I was a little girl I cared deeply what my parents thought. I wanted to make them happy, so I didn't often get into trouble. Because of this, the need for forgiveness really wasn't part of my thinking. As I became an adult, I assumed that life would be carefree. I thought all people were kind and easily pleased. *Did I lead a sheltered life, or what?* I dreamed the fairytale of living happily ever after. I honestly thought that was the way life would be. I married my first real boyfriend and high school sweetheart. I was totally smitten and believed that our love would conquer all. My gut told me that our differences needed to be addressed, but I was young and in love. That's all that mattered to me at the time. I felt certain that everything would be okay. However, everything wasn't okay. In truth, my life was very different from what I had imagined.

After my marriage ended nearly ten years later, I was devastated. The pain and grief I experienced was immeasurable. I felt unlovely, unwanted, unjust, and most of all, unforgivable. In my eyes I was tarnished. Although I did not even feel worthy to cry out to God, I remember grasping for His presence. My mind played and replayed the "if only" record—if only I had been this or that, or done this or that. My heart was convinced I had created a wall that God would not want to climb. I believed the lie that in the eyes of Jesus I was washed up, divorced, and miles from His grace.

I reasoned that since God hates divorce (Malachi 2:16), He hated me. Then one day I read Ephesians 1:7–8: "In him we have redemption through his blood, the forgiveness of sins, in accordance with the riches of God's grace that he lavished on us with all wisdom and understanding." At that moment I knew that the God who had walked through my darkest times was still with me. He had forgiven me and had already begun restoring me to walk in freedom.

Although our life has been infected with sin, and we have made our share of mistakes, it is never too late to get free of our past. We can come boldly to God and ask for His forgiveness. And in receiving His forgiveness, we will be set free. Indeed the *only* way to that freedom is through forgiveness. It is a vital necessity of life.

****

As you begin to pray for yourself, be courageous. Accepting God's forgiveness fully requires bravery on your part, but know that He longs to forgive and heal you.

Dear heavenly Father,

When I look at my life, I see a broken vessel. I have made mistakes that carry huge consequences. But today, Father, I ask that You forgive me. My heart breaks because of sadness and regret.
I ask You, Lord, to

- wipe away my sins and to cleanse me from all the unrighteousness. I confess to You my deepest secrets and ask You to forgive me for _____ (name your sins).
- bring to my mind those bad behaviors that I have done to offend You and others. (Take time to be quiet and listen for the Holy Spirit to speak to your heart.)
- forgive me for falling short in my marriage.
- forgive me for saying damaging words that have been hurtful to my family members, to my spouse (or former spouse), and to my children. I realize now that Your Word says that "words of the reckless pierce like swords, but the tongue of the wise brings healing" (Proverbs 12:18). Help me to bring healing from this day on.
- forgive me for shifting the blame for my shortcomings and for not taking responsibility for what I have said or done.
- forgive me for the misdeeds that I have thought or wished. I know that these offenses bring dishonor to You.
- forgive me for the things that I have done to cause pain to others, either unintentionally or intentionally.
- forgive me for not trusting You during my trials and for retaliating in anger.
- remind me every day that I can trust You.

Thank You for forgiving me and setting me free.

Thank You that Your forgiveness cleanses my heart and brings reconciliation between You and me. Thank You for Your amazing grace and mercy on my life.
I am humbled that You would love me so much.

In Jesus' name I pray, Amen.

Scriptures to Live By

Psalm 103:1–5
Praise the LORD, O my soul;
all my inmost being, praise his holy name.
Praise theLORD, O my soul,
and forget not all his benefits—
who forgives all your sins
and heals all your diseases,
who redeems your life from the pit
and crowns you with love and compassion,
who satisfies your desires with good things
so that your youth is renewed like the eagle's.

Micah 7:18–19
Who is a God like you,
who pardons sin and forgives the transgression
of the remnant of his inheritance?
You do not stay angry forever
but delight to show mercy.
You will again have compassion on us;
you will tread our sins underfoot
and hurl all our iniquities into the depths of the sea.

Matthew 6:12
"Forgive us our debts,
as we also have forgiven our debtors."

Matthew 6:14–15
"For if you forgive men when they sin against you, your heavenly Father will also forgive you. But if you do not forgive men their sins, your Father will not forgive your sins."

Ephesians 1:7–8
In him we have redemption through his blood, the forgiveness of sins, in accordance with the riches of God's grace that he lavished on us with all wisdom and understanding.

Colossians 1:13–14
For he has rescued us from the dominion of darkness and brought us into the kingdom of the Son he loves, in whom we have redemption, the forgiveness of sins.

Acts 5:31
God exalted him to his own right hand as Prince and Savior that he might give repentance and forgiveness of sins to Israel.

2

Help Me to Forgive

> Therefore, as God's chosen people, holy and dearly
> loved, clothe yourselves with compassion, kindness,
> humility, gentleness and patience. Bear with each other
> and forgive whatever grievances you may have against
> one another.
> Forgive as the Lord forgave you.
> —Colossians 3:12–13

Forgive: to stop being angry with someone; to stop blaming; to stop trying to punish

Forgiving is a hard task. In the previous chapter we talked about how difficult it sometimes is to feel that we have *received* forgiveness. Now, it's our turn to *give* it. We know in our head that we must forgive, yet our heart screams with protest because, in forgiving, we must also let go of the offense. After all, what good will it do to say we forgive someone while holding a grudge against them? We need help.

Forgiveness is a choice that acts like an emotion. One obstacle is that we tend to think that if we forgive someone, it lets him or her off the hook. But in actuality, it lets *us* off the hook. Forgiveness frees the forgiver. The one being forgiven, the offender, rarely realizes the need to be forgiven. Let go of all the expectations on the other person and you will become free to be who God created you to be. Trust God and allow Him to help you forgive.

During my separation and impending divorce, my two young children and I were living with my parents. It was a very trying time because I went from being a stay-at-home mom to working full time. In addition, my parents had an elderly parent with Alzheimer's living with them. So, not only did I feel sad and depressed because of the failure of my marriage, I felt despair from moving in with my parents who had their hands full already.

I tried to stay focused as I worked to provide a new life for my children and me, but it didn't take long for me to realize my need for steadfast prayer. I had to become constant and purposeful in how I prayed. In fact, my prayer life became the anchor to my emotions.

My soon-to-be ex-husband, on the other hand, appeared carefree and happy in his new role as a single person. He boasted about all the things he was doing and buying, including a sports car, yet refused to contribute to child support until the divorce was final and he would be legally required to do so.

For months I struggled in a state of shock and disbelief. When I asked him for help with necessary expenses for the children or questioned his intentions, he only laughed at me. His arrogance was overwhelming and my grip on trying to forgive him went right out the window. I was so angry. I felt hopeless and alone, so I prayed. I vented to the Lord how unfair this was. How could he say he had no money to help pay for diapers and then flaunt his extravagant lifestyle? I never understood this. He took very little active role in parenting and, in fact, was bold enough to tell me that I deserved the situation I was in. He denied any responsibility for the path we were on.

Not long after the divorce, it became evident that any discipline or rule setting for the children would be entirely on me. Yet any boundary I set, such as prohibiting certain television shows or movies, he intentionally allowed the kids to cross. They would return home from spending time with him and admit that he had allowed and even encouraged such incidents. Although I would burn with anger and disbelief inside, I knew I had a choice to make. I could retaliate with a verbal opinion, which is what I wanted to do, or I could restate my rules and expectations. I chose, only by God's help, the latter. Although I felt helpless, this led me straight to my knees in prayer. It was during these everyday moments that God taught me the power of prayer.

I am telling you this story to emphasize my need—and my responsibility—to forgive my former husband. This has been difficult to do many times. Often I have not felt that I could do it, but I would bring myself to say the words, "Lord, I don't know how, but I am choosing to forgive him," even though I didn't feel like forgiving him. But over time it has become easier. Do I still grieve over complicated situations? Yes. But I have learned to let go of the anger and the drive to retaliate.

Now, nearly twenty years later, God has healed those painful emotions and feelings of hurt and betrayal. I believe that through my prayer and constant conversation with the Lord, I won the battle with anger and resentment. I felt Him with me every step of the way. God became my companion and I experienced a peace unlike anything I have ever felt. God's grace and forgiveness are working through me.

****

I encourage you to trust the Father in heaven enough to forgive your offender. I leaned on a powerful scripture in Romans 12:19: "Do not take revenge, my friends, but leave room for God's wrath, for it is written: 'It is mine to avenge; I will repay,' says the Lord." The Lord's wrath is more just than yours, so trust Him with your sorrows. Forgive and let go of the outcome.

Dear heavenly Father,

The emotions and experiences I carry are filled with hurt and disappointment. I ask that You help me to
- release the burdens. In doing this, I know I must start with forgiveness.
- forgive every single person that has offended or hurt me. I realize that unforgiveness creates a barrier between You and me.
- not rely on my emotions but to do what's right even when I do not *feel* like doing it.
- expect the healing power of Your forgiveness in my own life.
- have compassion and gentleness with others because of what You have given to me.
- let go of the hurt and pain that I feel.
- confess to You my fears because I am choosing to forgive __(name the person)__ for __(name the offense)__.

Thank You, Lord, that through Your power, I am able to forgive. Even when I do not *feel* the forgiveness, I thank You that, according to Your Word, I can forgive. I realize that my feelings are unpredictable, and I must only rely on what I know to be true from Your Word. Thank You for bringing to my mind the offenses that I am holding onto so that I can release them to You
Thank You that when I forgive someone, I am also set free.
Thank You for teaching me this life-altering lesson.

This journey is hard, Lord, so I desperately need Your strength, and I thank You for it.
In Jesus' name I pray, Amen.

Scriptures to Live By

Matthew 6:14–15
"For if you forgive men when they sin against you, your heavenly Father will also forgive you. But if you do not forgive men their sins, your
Father will not forgive your sins."

Matthew 18:21–22
Then Peter came to Jesus and asked, "Lord, how many times shall I forgive my brother when he sins against me? Up to seven times?" Jesus answered, "I tell you, not seven times, but seventy-seven times."

Matthew 18:35
"This is how my heavenly Father will treat each of you unless you forgive your brother from your heart."

Mark 11:25
"And when you stand praying, if you hold anything against anyone, forgive him, so that your Father in heaven may forgive you your sins."

Luke 6:37
"Do not judge, and you will not be judged. Do not condemn, and you will not be condemned. Forgive, and you will be forgiven."

2 Corinthians 2:7
Now instead, you ought to forgive and comfort him, so that he will not be overwhelmed by excessive sorrow.

3

Renew My Heart

> Create in me a pure heart, O God,
> and renew a steadfast spirit within me.
> —Psalm 51:10

Renew: to put new things into my heart and mind; to change my thinking
Steadfast: the ability to stand strong in the midst of storms

Sometimes we don't recognize our own shortcomings; we don't always see our need for change. Our lives encounter so many distractions that our hearts go numb. In our noisy world of technology and social media, the allure of them has become an addiction that has taken over our thoughts. We need a spiritual and emotional renewal now more than ever. And how can that come about? I believe that the key is prayer.

In Psalm 51, David asked God to renew his spirit, to put new things into his heart and mind. He recognized the need for a change of thinking and called out to God in humility, *Lord, look at my heart and change me, and then make my renewed heart steadfast.* This is a sweet example of how to invite and embrace a new way of thinking; your mindset will change as you ask God to create inside of you a pure heart and to give you a steadfast spirit.

My oldest child, Kristin, is precious and beautiful inside and out. However, during her teenage years, she really struggled with anger, bitterness, and rebellion. Those were some of my most interesting years as a single parent. (If you have a teenager, you undoubtedly feel my pain.) My daughter was determined to get her way in most situations. One particular event comes to mind.

After six months of living with her dad in another city, Kristin decided to move back home with me. Her decision to leave my home in the first place was made with haste and in anger toward me, yet I knew I needed to let her go. Although it did not turn out to be all that she imagined, it was an important part of her journey.

As one can expect, it was an extremely difficult time in my life. Once again, I was driven to my knees in prayerful surrender. (The Lord often brings us back to the cross, doesn't He —back to that place where our relationship with Him first began, where He took our sins and sorrows upon Himself.) So I pursued God and His Word with all my might. My daughter had been living five hours away in an unhealthy environment. But God moved. One day, after much prayer and many tears on my part, she called and asked to move back home. Inside I was jumping up and down and praising the Lord, but still outwardly, I had to remain steadfast.

There was a spiritual and emotional storm still brewing between us. I told Kristin that while I longed for her to come home, I would require three things from her: obedience, submissiveness, and respect. Those were three areas where she had resisted most, and I had decided their end had come. You see, during the time she was gone, I had gained a new perspective and new strength. God had used that time to renew my spirit. I had been heartbroken over the issues between us when she had left, and that caused me to press into God.

I needed Him desperately then during the storm to renew a right spirit within my heart, and I need Him now, when the seas are calm. Kristin returned shortly after that conversation. She struggled at first because she didn't know how to react to this stronger person that her mom was becoming, but later she admitted that she respected me for it. I was more calm and self-assured, and she noticed. Our relationship began to change for the better, and today we are closer than we have ever been.

I had been looking for all the changes to come about in my child's life, but God changed me too. He uses the difficult or sorrowful times in our lives to make us stronger. So, be diligent to pray for a pure heart and steadfast spirit even during the most painful circumstances, and then watch the Lord change you from the inside out.

****

As you pray for a pure heart and a steadfast spirit, know that God is about to do a beautiful thing inside of you. He does not intend to give you a better version of yourself but to create in you a version of Himself. We are created in the image of His son and He longs to fill us with more of Him so that we acknowledge where our strength comes from.

Dear heavenly Father,

You alone know my heart. You know my every thought and You know my spirit. I ask according to Your Word that You create in me a pure heart and renew a right spirit within me.

I ask You Lord to

- create in me a willing spirit that will sustain me and keep me steadfast.
- help me to accept Your Word that is so powerful and life changing.
- pour Your Spirit into me that I may see You more clearly, and that my mind would be renewed.

Thank You, Father, for changing my heart.
Thank You for a renewed Spirit where my hopes are restored.
Thank You that my life is in Your hands. I trust in You and Your wonderful plans for me and for my children.
Jesus, I thank You for Your blood that You shed on the cross for me, that I may live a new life and be free of shame and guilt.
Thank You for the new thoughts and new desires You have poured into me.

In Jesus' name I pray, Amen.

Scriptures to Live By

Psalm 51:10–12
Create in me a pure heart, O God,
and renew a steadfast spirit within me.
Do not cast me from your presence
or take your Holy Spirit from me.
Restore to me the joy of your salvation
and grant me a willing spirit, to sustain me.

Romans 12:2
Do not conform any longer to the pattern of this world, but be transformed by the renewing of your mind. Then you will be able to test and approve what God's will is—his good, pleasing and perfect will.

Romans 15:13
May the God of hope fill you with all joy and peace as you trust in him, so that you may overflow with hope by the power of the Holy Spirit.

2 Corinthians 4:16
Therefore we do not lose heart. Though outwardly we are wasting away, yet inwardly we are being renewed day by day.

Colossians 3:8–17
But now you must rid yourselves of all such things as these: anger, rage, malice, slander, and filthy language from your lips. Do not lie to each other, since you have taken off your old self with its practices and have put on the new self, which is being renewed in knowledge in the image of its Creator. Here there is no Greek or Jew, circumcised or uncircumcised, barbarian, Scythian, slave or free, but
Christ is all, and is in all.

Therefore, as God's chosen people, holy and dearly loved, clothe yourselves with compassion, kindness, humility, gentleness and patience. Bear with each other and forgive whatever grievances you may have against one another. Forgive as the Lord forgave you. And over all these virtues put on love, which binds them all together in perfect unity.

Let the peace of Christ rule in your hearts, since as members of one body you were called to peace. And be thankful. Let the word of Christ dwell in you richly as you teach and admonish one another with all wisdom, and as you sing psalms, hymns and spiritual songs with gratitude in your hearts to God. And whatever you do, whether in word or deed, do it all in the name of the Lord Jesus, giving thanks to God the Father through him.

4

Give Me Peace

> The LORD gives strength to his people;
> the LORD blesses his people with peace.
> —Psalm 29:11

Peace: to not worry or fret, to remain calm, freedom of the mind from annoyance, distraction, or anxiety

Our Lord has called us to lead a life of peace, yet the perfectly peaceful life is not guaranteed. We will most definitely have struggles. So then, peace is something we must choose and strive for. But how do we do that? I believe there is an action we must take by choosing to trust God, who knows far more than we do. After all, our heavenly Father did not intend for us to feel stressed and anxious each day. On numerous occasions the Bible speaks of having peace. For example, Proverbs 14:30 reads, "A heart at peace gives life to the body." It is vital that we pursue peace—vital to our hearts and minds, as well as to our flesh and bones.

I am a worrier. I tend to fret over many things that never come to pass. My dad passed away suddenly while he and my mom were on vacation. He was only sixty-nine. For many years following his death, I would become instantly afraid when I could not get in contact with a loved one. So many scenarios would enter my mind and I would be worried that someone else has died suddenly. To be honest, I lived in near-constant fear. In my spirit the Lord tried to speak to me about this many times, but I just chose to worry instead. Then one day I was deeply convicted of my worry. The truth became clear to me that it was a sin. I repented, and the Lord is healing me and changing me, even as I write this book, but the healing started with my willingness to admit my weakness and trust God with it.

As I have begun the process of overcoming this issue and having freedom over it, I recognize a new strength that indeed comes from the peace of God. Although some fear is reasonable, such as a parent's instinct to protect her child, most fear and worry is indeed sin. We must train ourselves and our children to recognize the difference between a lack of trust in God and a sensible reaction to threatening situations. We must let go of anxiety and seek to have a heart of peace.

****

As you seek God for a peace that passes all understanding, meaning that it will not make sense to the world around you, know that you will find rest in God. Your perspective on all of life will change.

Dear heavenly Father,

I long to rest in You. "As the deer pants for streams of water, so my soul pants for you, O God" (Psalm 42:1–2). I pray

- for peace that passes all understanding.
- for a new strength and a blessing on my life. Lord, Your Word says that You will give strength to Your people and that You will bless Your people with peace (Psalm 29:11).
- that You would cover me with peace that comes from Your Holy Spirit. I confess that sometimes I do not feel peaceful, but I choose to stand on the knowledge of Your power, not on my feelings.
- that I would remember Your simple truth that I can trust You because You love me.

Thank You for the blessing of Your peace.
Thank You that Your Word brings peace to my heart. I lay my troubled heart at Your feet because I know that letting go of my burden allows me to hold onto You.
Thank You for settling down my spirit this very moment and for giving peace to my soul.

In Jesus' name I pray, Amen.

Scriptures to Live By

Psalm 29:11
The LORD gives strength to his people;
the LORD blesses his people with peace.

Psalm 42:1
As the deer pants for streams of water,
so my soul pants for you, O God.

Psalm 62:5
Find rest, O my soul, in God alone;
my hope comes from him.

Proverbs 14:30
A heart at peace gives life to the body,
but envy rots the bones.

Matthew 11:28–30
"Come to me, all you who are weary and burdened, and
I will give you rest. Take my yoke upon you and learn
from me, for I am gentle and humble in heart, and you
will find rest for your souls. For my yoke is easy and my
burden is light."

Philippians 4:4–7
Rejoice in the Lord always. I will say it again: Rejoice.
Let your gentleness be evident to all. The Lord is near.
Do not be anxious about anything, but in everything, by
prayer and petition, with thanksgiving, present your
requests to God. And the peace of God, which
transcends all understanding, will guard your hearts
and your minds in Christ Jesus.

Philippians 4:8–9
Finally, brothers, whatever is true, whatever is noble,
whatever is right, whatever is pure, whatever is lovely,
whatever is admirable—if anything is excellent or
praiseworthy—think about such things. Whatever you

have learned or received or heard from me, or seen in
me—put it into practice. And the
God of peace will be with you.

Philippians 4:10–13
I rejoice greatly in the Lord that at last you have
renewed your concern for me. Indeed, you have been
concerned, but you had no opportunity to show it. I am
not saying this because I am in need, for I have learned
to be content whatever the circumstances. I know what
it is to be in need, and I know what it is to have plenty.
I have learned the secret of being content in any and
every situation, whether well fed or hungry, whether
living in plenty or in want. I can do
everything through him who gives me strength.

5

Humble Me

> Be completely humble and gentle;
> be patient, bearing with one another in love.
> —Ephesians 4:2

Humble: to be meek or modest, not arrogant, to put others before yourself; to admit that you need God and His help in your life

Jesus said in Matthew 23:12, "For whoever exalts himself will be humbled, and whoever humbles himself will be exalted." This means we have a choice. If we do not become humble, then God will take it upon Himself to cause that change in us. Humility is important to God because He knows it is vital to success in our relationships. Many friendships are ruined because one person fails to recognize his or her need for the other, or disregards the need to change when the relationship has been damaged. This is regrettable because reconciliation can often occur through a simple admission that one person has hurt the other, followed by a sincere apology for causing them pain. This ability and willingness to seek reconciliation is a true sign of humility.

Humility goes hand in hand with peace. If we humble ourselves and have a loving, merciful, and gracious attitude toward people, it allows God to work. Our heart becomes fashioned like Jesus and there is room for the blessings that God wants to give through us.

Take a moment to consider what is really in your heart. For example, are you often arrogant and self-centered, considering only what is best for you? Are you ever condescending toward others or acting with intent to intimidate? Do not be mistaken, God sees and knows all that is in our heart, and He will discipline His children. Decide today to make the necessary adjustments before God steps in to bring them about.

My children, who are now adults, are aware of my inability to live without peace between us. I have said "I'm sorry" more times than I care to remember. Although the majority of those apologies were warranted, some were given only to make peace. I believe that sometimes you must do whatever is necessary to open up the lines of communication and allow healing to begin.

One particular occasion came during a counseling session with my daughter and her therapist, where I needed to humble myself and apologize. She was very angry with me over my divorce. She had no concern about the causes, she just needed to hear me say "I am sorry." As I sat there, listening to my daughter pour out her heart, I searched for what to say. In my thinking, I could only apologize for causing her pain, not for the actual act of the divorce. I had lived with emotional and verbal abuse that she did not yet understand and that I hoped she would never experience. I knew that I must stand on my decision without explaining my issue.

The Lord taught me a valuable lesson that day. You see, my flesh wanted to lash out and defend myself. I was actually feeling angry and I wanted to justify my actions. But God silenced me in that moment and all I could think to say was, "I am so sorry that I caused you pain." The truth was that my action did cause great pain, justified or not, and I was indeed sorry for that.

The Lord began to heal me by showing me how to respond with humility and grace during the most painful moments. On this particular day, as I sat face-to-face with my brokenhearted teenage daughter, I was forced to make a decision. Would I give in to self-centeredness and defend myself, or respond with humility and grace so that my sweet child could begin to experience God's healing along with me? Thankfully, with much prayer and again by God's grace, I let go of my emotion and allowed God to move. Shortly after this episode, I began to notice a heaviness lift from Kristin's life. It was as though she needed to hear my sorrow over what affected her and then see God working in my life.

****

Seek humility with all of your heart and mind. As you begin to pray, confess your arrogance, selfishness, and pride. Remember that God already knows. Be encouraged because God promises grace and honor to the humble (1 Peter 5:5–6). That is worth the trade-off!

Dear heavenly Father,

I confess my wall of pride has been building over the years, and I ask from You today

- forgiveness for thinking that I can handle my life without You. I know now that not seeking Your will in my life exemplifies my prideful heart.
- to break down the wall of pride.
- to forgive my prideful heart and show me how to put aside my own ways and trust in Your ways.
- to help me every day to surrender my will to Your will.
- to help me honor You with a spirit of humility so that I can be transformed day by day.
- that I would start to live my life according to Ephesians 4:2, being completely humble and gentle; being patient and bearing others in love.

Thank You for showing me this life-changing truth.
Thank You for the humility that I am learning.
Thank You for giving me the desire to put the needs of other people before my own.

I love You, trust You and need You. In Jesus' name I pray, Amen.

Scriptures to Live By

2 Chronicles 7:14
"If my people, who are called by my name, will humble themselves and pray and seek my face and turn from their wicked ways, then will I hear from heaven and will forgive their sin and will heal their land."

Psalm 25:9
He guides the humble in what is right
and teaches them his way.

Ephesians 4:2
Be completely humble and gentle; be patient, bearing
with one another in love.

Titus 3:1–2
Remind the people to be subject to rulers and
authorities, to be obedient, to be ready to do whatever
is good, to slander no one, to be peaceable and
considerate, and to show true humility toward all men.

1 Peter 3:8
Finally, all of you, live in harmony with one another; be
sympathetic, love as brothers, be compassionate and
humble.

1 Peter 5:5–6
Young men, in the same way be submissive to those
who are older. All of you, clothe yourselves with
humility toward one another, because, "God opposes
the proud but gives grace to the humble." Humble
yourselves, therefore, under God's mighty hand, that he
may lift you up in due time.

James 4:6
But he gives us more grace. That is why Scripture says:
"God opposes the proud but gives grace to the
humble."

Matthew 23:12
"For whoever exalts himself will be humbled, and
whoever humbles
himself will be exalted."

6

Remove the Loneliness

*And my God will meet all your needs, according to
his glorious riches in Christ Jesus.*
—Philippians 4:19

Loneliness: to feel sadness because you are alone

God never intended for us to be alone. We are created for relationship, especially with Him. But this innate desire for personal connections often leads us to make poor decisions. For example, we might plunge hastily into a relationship for the sole purpose of simply having someone to be with. Unfortunately, the eventual results are usually painful and ugly. The price we pay is more than we could have ever dreamed. Nonetheless, God can use personal crises to bring about change in us, causing us to first evaluate our relationship with Him. This is a good thing.

Shortly after I became a single mom, my precious sister Jeri reminded me that the Lord Himself is my helper. She encouraged me, on more than one occasion, to lean on the Lord emotionally and spiritually as I would imagine leaning on my husband in a healthy relationship. At first, I didn't understand this concept, but over time God made it clear. I learned to turn to Him at every moment and with every issue that I would have shared with my spouse. In other words, during those times when I began to feel lonely, I would start to pray and talk to the Lord about the issue at hand. As one spouse would typically converse with the other and say, "I have this going on, what do you think I should do?" This is exactly how I would talk with God. I learned to converse with the Lord about everything!

My explanation here does not give due accolades to my Savior; nonetheless, this practice proved to be an amazing way to encounter Him. Did I long for human companionship? Certainly, yes I did. Yet as I became stronger in who I was in Christ, God was changing me. During those years I learned many important things about myself. I discovered that I had codependent tendencies, a negative perception of who I was, and a discontentment over my marital status. These were unhealthy mindsets that needed to be broken, and God was at work doing just that.

Through constant prayerful communication with the Lord, my way of thinking changed. When you hang out with someone long enough, you begin to think like them, and understand their thoughts and plans a little more clearly. I learned that God still had a purpose for my life. I learned that He always hears my prayer, and that He will never leave me. I also learned that even though I was alone, I didn't have to be lonely. The security of being someone's wife was replaced with the security of being God's child.

****

Being alone can be difficult, but also positively life changing. I encourage you to grab the hand of your heavenly Father and walk with Him during the hardest moments of your life. Then, when those hard times are over, you'll notice that your death-grip has loosened to a gentle clasp of your dependable Father's hand. You are developing a dependency on God that will carry you to the end. He is showing you what you've needed for a long time.

Dear heavenly Father,

I am lonely, and I confess this to You. I also confess to You

- that this singleness is uncomfortable to me.
- my past discontentment has caused me to make decisions that were not Your will.
- that I need to clear my mind of the untrue thought that other people are somehow responsible to meet my needs and make me happy.
- that I need You in my life first and foremost before I can consider another relationship.
- that I need You to remind me every day of these truths.
- my loneliness and ask that You remove it and fill me with Your presence.

Thank You for showing me what I need.
Thank You for showing me things about myself.
Thank You for helping me to surrender my heart to You.
Thank You for helping me to know You in a deeper way.
Thank You for the good plan that You still have for me.
Thank You for taking away my loneliness.
Thank You for complete contentment.
Thank You for Your promise to meet all of my needs.

In Jesus' name, I pray, Amen.

Scriptures to Live By

Psalm 25:16
Turn to me and be gracious to me,
for I am lonely and afflicted.

Psalm 62:1–2
My soul finds rest in God alone; my salvation comes
from him. He alone is my rock and my salvation; he is
my fortress, I will never be shaken

Psalm 63:1–5
O God, you are my God,
earnestly I seek you;
my soul thirsts for you,
my body longs for you,
in a dry and weary land
where there is no water.

I have seen you in the sanctuary
and beheld your power and your glory.
Because your love is better than life,
my lips will glorify you.
I will praise you as long as I live,
and in your name I will lift up my hands.
My soul will be satisfied as with the richest of foods;
with singing lips my mouth will praise you.

2 Corinthians 4:9
We are hard pressed on every side …
cuted, but not abandoned; struck down, but not
destroyed.

Philippians 4:11
I am not saying this because I am in need, for I have learned
to be content whatever the circumstances.

Philippians 4:19
And my God will meet all your needs according to
his glorious riches in Christ Jesus.

7

Give Me Wisdom

> If any of you lacks wisdom, he should ask God, who
> gives generously
> to all without finding fault, and it will be given to him.
> —James 1:5

Wisdom: knowing what to do, having good judgment, being able to discern

One definition of *wisdom* emphasizes scholarly knowledge or learning. This is what the world considers most important, but God says differently. He instructs us to ask for *His* wisdom, by which we can achieve great things, make right decisions, and fulfill the destiny He has placed within us. Ask God for wisdom and He will give you more than you can imagine.

When looking back at many of the decisions I've made, I do not feel like a wise person. Often I hear myself saying, "What was I thinking? I should have done this or that." Hindsight always clears up our view, doesn't it? But anyone can judge his or her past; the real test is in how we face our future.

God knows we need wisdom. This is why He said that if we lack wisdom, He will generously give it (James 1:5).

When it came to my children, I was quick to rely on God's wisdom over my own. I knew I didn't have all the answers. After all, I was single and raising two precious people alone, so I had to pray fervently and depend on Him to help me. He was the "eyes in the back of my head," as the saying goes. My children now joke about how I always knew when they were just about to get into trouble, sneak out, or make a bad decision. Many times I would wake up in the middle of the night to check on them just in time. And I always seemed to know when they were in serious trouble. Some call that freaky luck. I call that the wisdom of God working through me.

When my son, Jason, was in the eighth and ninth grades, he was pursued by classmates who concerned me. I believe now that the battle was spiritual. He was constantly approached by other students who wanted him to join their parties, which always included sex, drugs, and alcohol. He would come home and talk about how a certain popular student wanted to pay him to be the life of a party (meaning, to do certain things upon their dare, things that were out of character for him). Jason was an athlete and loved by his coaches. He stood out for his hard work and successes. I believe that the enemy was pursuing him with the intent to make him fail. The Bible warns us in John 10:10 that our enemy, Satan, comes to steal, kill, and destroy. It seemed obvious to me that the enemy wanted to destroy Jason and his reputation. Even more obvious was how much I needed to pray over him.

Fortunately and unfortunately, Jason witnessed some bad choices made by a close friend in whom those very experiences and consequences gave Jason wisdom for his own life. Yet, he was still being pressured by other popular kids to join in their "fun." We talked about it a lot, and I continued to remind him that God had given him unique wisdom and perspective. As a parent, I prayed and prayed for wisdom on how to handle this. I could not be with him every second of the day, so he had to make good decisions on his own. And to be honest, I worried about it. So I poured as much wisdom as I could into his young heart and mind. I reminded him that he could either follow God's way and be under his protection, and therefore be happy and blessed, or he could follow other students and face the consequences.

Thankfully, he did choose to ignore those students, and not so surprisingly, they eventually gave up pursuing him. Jason learned the value of heeding advice from his mom, and I once again discovered the value of prayer, pressing into God's Word, and trusting the wisdom of the Lord.

****

Proverbs is full of God's wisdom, and its thirty-one chapters make it easy to read one each day of the month. Every day take in God's Word and discover the difference it will make in your life. And as you pray for God's wisdom, be encouraged that He will give it to you. Trust that quiet discerning thought or feeling inside of you. It will change your life.

Dear heavenly Father,

I need You. Your Word says in James 1:5 that if I ask for wisdom, You will give it to me without reproach. Yet, I understand that I must seek You with all my heart and incline my heart to Your voice. Help me to do this. I pray

- to follow You and Your ways from this day forward.
- to discover Your wisdom as You will guard my path and be my shield.
- forgive me for my past foolishness. Today, I choose You.
- help me to gain wisdom and understanding, and to hold them close to my heart and mind.

Thank You for the blessings in my life that I receive when I listen to You.
Thank You for Your Word and the instructions You give.
Thank You for helping me let go of my own arrogance, thinking that my way is better.
Thank You for pursuing me and being patient as I learn to trust Your wisdom.

In Jesus' name I pray, Amen.

Scriptures to Live By

Psalm 143:10–12
Teach me to do your will,
for you are my God;
may your good Spirit
lead me on level ground.

For your name's sake, O LORD, preserve my life;
in your righteousness, bring me out of trouble.
In your unfailing love, silence my enemies;

destroy all my foes,
for I am your servant.

Proverbs 2

My son, if you accept my words
and store up my commands within you,
turning your ear to wisdom
and applying your heart to understanding,
and if you call out for insight
and cry aloud for understanding,
and if you look for it as for silver
and search for it as for hidden treasure,
then you will understand the fear of the LORD
and find the knowledge of God.
For the LORD gives wisdom,
and from his mouth come knowledge and understanding.
He holds victory in store for the upright,
he is a shield to those whose walk is blameless,
for he guards the course of the just
and protects the way of his faithful ones.

Then you will understand what is right and just
and fair—every good path.
For wisdom will enter your heart,
and knowledge will be pleasant to your soul.
Discretion will protect you,
and understanding will guard you.

Wisdom will save you from the ways of wicked men,
from men whose words are perverse,
who leave the straight paths
to walk in dark ways,
who delight in doing wrong
and rejoice in the perverseness of evil,
whose paths are crooked
and who are devious in their ways.

It will save you also from the adulteress,
from the wayward wife with her seductive words,
who has left the partner of her youth
and ignored the covenant she made before God.

For her house leads down to death
and her paths to the spirits of the dead.
None who go to her return
or attain the paths of life.

Thus you will walk in the ways of good men
and keep to the paths of the righteous.
For the upright will live in the land,
and the blameless will remain in it;
but the wicked will be cut off from the land,
and the unfaithful will be torn from it.

Proverbs 3:13–20
Blessed is the man who finds wisdom,
the man who gains understanding,
for she is more profitable than silver
and yields better returns than gold.
She is more precious than rubies;
nothing you desire can compare with her.
Long life is in her right hand;
in her left hand are riches and honor.
Her ways are pleasant ways,
and all her paths are peace.

She is a tree of life to those who embrace her;
those who lay hold of her will be blessed.

By wisdom the LORD laid the earth's foundations,
by understanding he set the heavens in place;
by his knowledge the deeps were divided,
and the clouds let drop the dew.

Proverbs 4:5
Get wisdom, get understanding;
do not forget my words or swerve from them.

Proverbs 24:3
By wisdom a house is built,
and through understanding it is established.

Luke 21:15

"For I will give you words and wisdom that none of
your adversaries
will be able to resist or contradict."

8

Bridle My Tongue

> The tongue has the power of life and death,
> and those who love it will eat its fruit.
> —Proverbs 18:21

Tongue: the instrument of our speech

Much trouble comes through the opening of our mouth. We all say things we shouldn't. Think for a minute: Would your conversation change if certain people were present? Would you give the same description about your work environment if your boss were standing next to you? Would you change your words if someone you wanted to impress were listening?

What about Jesus? He is the one that judges our thoughts and actions, and He *is* with us. Yet we forget this and use our words dangerously, as we carelessly express our every thought and feeling. I am often guilty of this, but I have learned through hard lessons that it is actually possible to keep my mouth shut.

It is satisfying and rewarding to remain silent when I have opportunity to lash out, have a witty comeback ready, or feel justified in speaking my mind. I have discovered that I feel more in control when I take a moment to be silent, and choose my words very carefully. It is liberating. As in all areas of life, we can develop good habits of speech; and silence may be the one we should work on first. I'm not saying we should never speak up in our defense, but instead to *carefully* respond. It is not necessary to say everything we are thinking.

We really do have the power in our tongue to either tear down or build up. I encourage you to be an encourager with your words. My mom used to say, "If you can't say anything nice, don't say anything at all." I think that most of the time those are good words to live by. When you must say something in your own defense, say it as kindly as you can.

I must admit that there have been times when I wanted the whole world to know how I had been wronged, abused, or mistreated. I especially wanted to blurt it out to my children. But I know in my heart that if I did, it would be with wrong intentions. Again, it took me back to my prayer life and allowing the Lord to silence me at the right moments so that my purpose was pure, and not self-seeking. We indeed may be justified to express the truth at some point, but I encourage you to be prayerful and use caution in the words you say and in choosing the right time for saying them.

Solomon wrote in Proverbs 15:1: "A gentle answer turns away wrath, but a harsh word stirs up anger." A quiet answer can calm down emotions and allow for reasonable conversation. In due time, your quiet spirit can win the battle against the injustice done to you because it leaves room for the Lord to show the truth in His perfect timing.

My ex-husband blames me for his hard life. To this day, our children are subjected to stories that slander my character and integrity. Thankfully, they both refuse to participate in those conversations. However, my daughter went through a two-year period of time in which she was extremely angry toward me because of the lies she was told. When she and I were finally able to discuss the issues, she realized the things being said did not line up. She questioned me for a long time and then compared my explanations to what she had been told. She needed to come to her own conclusions based on the facts.

I was angry when this conversation started, wrestling in my heart with the Spirit of the Lord. I wanted to yell out the truth and empty all the junk from my child's mind; I felt I would be justified in doing so. Nonetheless, God had a different plan. Because He loves me, He pursued me and covered me with His righteousness in that moment. By His grace He bridled my tongue and kept me from using harsh words to defend myself.

This lesson was extremely difficult, but God continued to remind me that He is the avenger, not me (Romans 12:17–19). He has avenged to a far greater degree than I could have ever done myself. Both of my children came to see the truth. I didn't have to convince them. I just had to wait and live out my life with honesty. I had to shut my mouth and allow the Lord to protect me and make things right.

****

God is loving, just, and righteous. Trust Him with your words. The way you speak can be a life changer for you and for your children.

Dear heavenly Father,

Your Word says in Proverbs 18:21, "The tongue has the power of life and death, and those who love it will eat its fruit." Help me to remember these truths, and I pray

- that I always remember that whatever I say will have consequences.
- that You will help me to bridle my tongue and control my speech. I confess that I have failed at keeping a guard on my lips in the past, and I ask You to remind me to guard my words.
- that You will remind me of the many wise teachings in Your holy Word concerning my tongue and how I choose to use my words. Help me. I cannot do this without You.
- that You will remind me to use my words wisely around my children. They need me to bridle my tongue and control my words. They need positive encouragement together with consistent answers as they study and learn from my actions and reactions.
- that You will give me a gentle answer when I need it.
- that I will be slow to anger and quick to forgive.
- that You would redefine my character and my tongue so that what I say will bring honor to You.

Thank You for dwelling in my home so that my family can receive life from the words You speak through me.
Thank You for giving me a quiet spirit that will stir in my kids the desire to be gentle also.
Thank You that through this change, my home will become a safe place for me, for my children, and for all who enter.

In Jesus' name I pray, Amen.

Scriptures to Live By

Proverbs 15:1–2
A gentle answer turns away wrath,
but a harsh word stirs up anger.

The tongue of the wise commends knowledge,
but the mouth of the fool gushes folly.

Proverbs 15:4
The tongue that brings healing is a tree of life,
but a deceitful tongue crushes the spirit.

Proverbs 18:21
The tongue has the power of life and death,
and those who love it will eat its fruit.

James 1:19
My dear brothers, take note of this: Everyone should be quick to listen,
slow to speak and slow to become angry.

James 3:5–8
Likewise the tongue is a small part of the body, but it makes great boasts. Consider what a great forest is set on fire by a small spark. The tongue also is a fire, a world of evil among the parts of the body. It corrupts the whole person, sets the whole course of his life on fire, and is itself set on fire by hell.

All kinds of animals, birds, reptiles and creatures of the sea are being tamed and have been tamed by man, but no man can tame the tongue. It is a restless evil, full of deadly poison.

9

Show Me How to Serve

> So if you faithfully obey the commands I am giving you today—to love the LORD your God and to serve him with all your heart and with all your soul—then I will send rain on your land in its season, both autumn and spring rains, so that you may gather in your grain, new wine and oil. I will provide grass in the fields of your cattle, and you will eat and be satisfied.
> —Deuteronomy 11:13–15

Serve: To do something for someone else, to do for others

The Lord wants us to have a servant's heart, where we naturally perform kind and gentle acts for other people. We do not have to work in the church to be a servant of the Lord; serving can amount to simple random acts of kindness, such as paying for a stranger's meal or seeing a need and stopping to help. Ask God today how you can serve Him in your community, on your job, and in your family.

As a single parent, it was difficult for me to find time to serve in my community or church. I had very little energy or time to volunteer on a regular basis. However, God's Word doesn't say, *if* you feel like it, serve one another. We are instructed many times to serve God, to serve others, and to be faithful in what God has given us (Matthew 24:45, 25:14–27). I knew that God longed for me to serve, and I also knew that when I serve others, I am serving Him. Galatians 5:13 reads, "You, my brothers, were called to be free. But do not use your freedom to indulge the sinful nature; rather, serve one another in love." This is an important message about our choices; we can choose to find ways to serve.

There came a point in my life when God began to convict me about serving others. My life was so hectic, I tried to ignore His voice. My sister Cindy sets such a wonderful example of a woman constantly looking for ways to serve. It was so refreshing to see the joy she received by helping others, so I asked the Lord to show me ways He wanted me to serve, even with my busy schedule. (God has a good reason for everything He asks us to do. He will give us the seed to sow, and we must sow that seed in the lives of others in order to receive the harvest in our own.)

As though God had been waiting for me to become willing, He opened my eyes to opportunities to serve people in my church, my coworkers, and my own children. At church, I joined a Care Ministry, ministering to those who had lost loved ones. At work, I found ways to encourage my peers. At home, I offered the idea to my kids to have "hang-out nights" for their friends to come over and play games and eat snacks. I would have some crazy loud weekend nights, but it was a safe place for my kids to hang out and an opportunity for me to serve and get to know their friends. I learned later that many of those teenagers were troubled and had no parent around, which may explain why they gravitated to my house.

I was inspired to know that God could and would still use me if I was willing. The reality is that our days go by quickly, and our sphere of influence will change as we age. Yet with every age, I am convinced that our best influence comes through serving others.

****

As you pray, ask the Lord to show you how to be obedient in this area. Be willing to get out of your comfort zone and meet the needs of someone else. It is extremely rewarding!

Dear heavenly Father,

When I read Your Word in Deuteronomy 11, I understand that I need to faithfully obey, to love You and serve You with all my heart. I see the connection between loving You and serving You. Therefore, I pray

- because Your Word tells me in Colossians 3:23 that whatever I do, I am supposed to do it for You, remind me to serve others in such a way that will bring glory to Your name.

- help me remember these principles every morning when I wake and every night as I lie down.
- show me what Your plan is for me and open up the doors of opportunity to serve.
- enable me to use what I have learned to minister to others who may be seeking You.
- give me the words to bring blessing to someone else.
- give me a heart to serve You with humility and grace, beginning in my own home.
- help me to remember the difference between a servant heart and a busy heart.

Thank You for the opportunity to serve You in whatever stage of life I am in.
Thank You for teaching me these principles day by day.

I love You. In Jesus' name I pray, Amen.

Scriptures to Live By

Deuteronomy 13:4
It is the LORD your God you must follow, and him you must revere. Keep his commands and obey him; serve him and hold fast to him.

Joshua 22:5
But be very careful to keep the commandment and the law that Moses the servant of the LORD gave you: to love the LORD your God, to walk in all his ways, to obey his commands, to hold fast to him and to serve him with all
your heart and all your soul.

Joshua 24:15
But if serving the LORD seems undesirable to you, then choose for yourselves this day whom you will serve, whether the gods your forefathers served beyond the

River, or the gods of the Amorites, in whose land you are living.
But as for me and my household, we will serve the LORD.

Matthew 6:24
"No one can serve two masters. Either he will hate the one and love the other, or he will be devoted to the one and despise the other. You cannot serve both God and Money."

Ephesians 6:7–8
Serve wholeheartedly, as if you were serving the Lord, not men, because you know that the Lord will reward everyone for whatever good he does, whether he is slave or free.

Colossians 3:23
Whatever you do, work at it with all your heart, as working for the Lord, not for men.

Colossians 4:5–6
Be wise in the way you act toward outsiders; make the most of every opportunity. Let your conversation be always full of grace, seasoned with salt, so that you may know how to answer everyone.

Hebrews 9:14
How much more, then, will the blood of Christ, who through the eternal Spirit offered himself unblemished to God, cleanse our consciences from acts that lead to death, so that we may serve the living God!

PART TWO

Praying for Your Children

Through the previous nine chapters, you have sought the Lord with your heart, soul, and mind to become the kind of prayer warrior the Holy Spirit is calling you to be. These next eleven chapters offer guidance for praying purposefully for your children. Most likely, they are confused and frightened as they face life with a broken family or a missing parent.

As you pray, focus on areas that are specific to each individual child, and ask God to show you things that you may not have realized before. You asked for wisdom in chapter seven, now trust God to give you that wisdom and discernment as you intercede for your child.

> Devote yourselves to prayer, being watchful and thankful.
> —Colossians 4:2

A Word of Encouragement for Parents

Our children are precious gifts from God, and He has made us accountable for their well-being. I believe that even as they grow into their own age of accountability, we can greatly influence their lives by our daily prayers.

I don't have to remind you that as a single parent, we may feel alone in this responsibility. However, God longs for you to rely on Him and hold on to His every word. Use the following section to enter the throne room of God with fervent prayers for your child. I encourage you to pray and then expect great changes in their hearts. Whether you see a change in a day or weeks, months, even years, God promises to intercede. Stay steadfast in your pursuit to see your child become the person God wants him to be. And most of all, remember that God is faithful.

10

Heal Their Broken Hearts

> He heals the brokenhearted
> and binds up their wounds.
> He determines the number of the stars
> and calls them each by name.
> Great in our Lord and mighty in power;
> his understanding has no limit.
> —Psalm 147:3–5

Broken: not functioning
Brokenhearted: extremely sad; overwhelmed by grief or despair

My own heart breaks when I think that my children's hearts have been broken, especially because to some degree, my divorce is the cause. I had a role in causing them pain.

If our children are living, or have ever lived, in a single parent home, they need healing. Their struggles are different from children in an intact family, and their wounds go deep. Each situation has its own set of troubling circumstances—the results of a broken home and an absent parent—but our God is faithful. He came to heal the brokenhearted, and He knows exactly what our children need.

My children are now twenty-two and twenty-six years old. It's been nearly twenty years since their father and I divorced, and they still have sadness over it. God has healed them in many ways, and they are now strong and independent; but down in the depths of their hearts, they of course wish things had turned out differently for our family. Children do not just "get over it" as some may think. Even understanding the reason does not take away the pain.

My daughter had some deep resentment as a teenager. However, God has healed her heart. She is married now and has learned to lean on her own husband, as well as her heavenly Father, for that empty place she longed to save for her dad. I have witnessed an amazing transformation in her heart and mind. She has blossomed into a beautiful woman of grace, mercy, and compassion. She is on the journey of total forgiveness and her life exemplifies that change.

My son, Jason, has an unwavering ability to accept those things he cannot change. He has been able to press on regardless of his unfavorable past, of missing out on a solid relationship with his biological father. Has it always been easy and victorious? Absolutely not. There were some very dark moments of pain, especially during his teenage years. On several occasions his father sent him long letters describing my failures and faults as a mother and wife in attempt to ruin Jason's opinion of me and to destroy our relationship. Although those attempts were unsuccessful, they brought great stress and sadness to this precious young man.

Needless to say, I was once again heartbroken on behalf of my child. I spent many nights on my knees before God, pleading for my son. I prayed that according Psalm 147:3, the Lord would heal Jason's broken heart and bind up his wounds. My child was sad and needed the Savior's touch. And once again, God answered. Jason has experienced God's healing in those dark places. His past contains memories of hurts, disappointments, and a turbulent relationship with his missing parent. Yet that is only his past, not his future. He has chosen to forgive his father and move on, living his life with honesty and integrity.

God has continued to pour out His kindness and love over my children. I praise Him for this. He has intervened in amazing ways to bring healing into our broken family. I am so thankful for a God who both saves and restores. God will encompass our children in such a way to empower them to live a glorious life. If you find your family in a similar situation, take courage that God knows and is working through all circumstances for His glory.

****

I encourage you to be watchful over your children's emotions. Pray fervently over them that God would heal their hurts, some of which you may never know about. But God knows, and He loves your child more than you can imagine.

Dear heavenly Father,

My child has been broken. The pain goes too deep for me to understand, but You do. You alone know everything that my child has thought, felt, experienced, and dreamed. I pray that

- in Jesus' name You would touch them.
- Your Holy Spirit would minister life back into their hearts.
- You would heal those areas that have been crushed and violated.
- my children will become whole again before any roots of bitterness, anger or resentment begin to take hold in their young hearts.
- You would protect them from further loss and brokenness.
- You would put Your wings of love around them to guard them from feelings of hurt, disillusionment, and rejection.

Thank You, Lord, for loving my children more that I could ever imagine.
Thank You that You have a good plan for my children's lives.
Thank You that today my children begin to feel whole again, and that peace and joy settles into their souls.
Thank You for being our healer.

In Jesus' name I pray, Amen.

Scriptures to Live By

2 Kings 20:5
"Go back and tell Hezekiah, the leader of my people, 'This is what the LORD, the God of your father David, says: I have heard your prayer and seen your tears; I will heal you. On the third day from now you will go up to the
temple of the LORD.'"

Psalm 30:2
O LORD my God, I called to you for help
and you healed me.

Psalm 103:2–5
Praise the LORD, O my soul,
and forget not all his benefits—
who forgives all your sins
and heals all your diseases,
who redeems your life from the pit
and crowns you with love and compassion,
who satisfies your desires with good things
so that your youth is renewed like the eagle's.

Psalm 147:3
He heals the brokenhearted
and binds up their wounds.

Isaiah 53:5
But he was pierced for our transgressions,
he was crushed for our iniquities;
the punishment that brought us peace was upon him,
and by his wounds we are healed.

James 5:16
Therefore confess your sins to each other and pray for each other so that you may be healed. The prayer of a righteous man is powerful and effective.

1 Peter 2:24
He himself bore our sins in his body on the tree, so that we might die to sins and live for righteousness; by his wounds you have been healed.

11

Give Them Peace

> And the peace of God, which transcends all understanding,
> will guard your hearts and your minds in Christ Jesus.
> —Philippians 4:7

Peace: freedom of the mind from annoyance, distraction, anxiety, or worry

We all need God's peace to calm our hearts and minds. However, children are so much more vulnerable. Adolescents are constantly bombarded with false messages regarding how to be happy. The near-constant pressure to fit in can lead to depression and destructive behaviors. Children from broken homes face additional challenges, often seeking to fill the void left by an absent parent in ways that only add to their pain.

These misconceptions about life are from the enemy. The truth is, God longs to fill those empty places in our children's hearts. He *yearns* to complete our children. Our heavenly Father knows exactly what they need, and this is why we need to intercede for them. Although we cannot deposit peace inside of them, we can create an environment of peace through the power of prayer.

I was not so great at this as I ran on high emotions most of the time. However, at the end of each day it was extremely important to me that both of the kids drift off to sleep with good and peaceful thoughts. We may have had turbulence earlier in the evening, but as they got into bed, I wanted to make sure they were okay, both emotionally and spiritually. I was purposeful to make sure we all were at peace before the lights went off. One at a time, I would climb onto their beds and draw them close to me, loving on them and saying I am sorry for being irritable or stressed out, or whatever the case was at the time. I would encourage them to apologize as well, if necessary, and then we would let it go. I would talk to them about their day, pray with them, and try my best to create that environment of peace before leaving their room.

I know that God helped me through those evenings by constant prayer, because I remembered also being so very emotional and fretful. But I was also hopeful that in some small way, they had peace in the midst of their trials.

****

Do not be restless as you petition the Lord for your children. Go boldly to God and allow Him to help you as you pray over them. God will honor your effort, regardless of how you feel at the moment.

Dear heavenly Father,

Thank You for giving me peace that is immeasurable and unexplainable. Your peace is not what the world gives, but an abundance of life that flows freely from you. In Jesus' name I ask You

- to bring peace to ___(mention each child by name)___. Your peace blesses their soul and restores their heart and mind.
- to comfort them and help them through the difficult journey they may be walking.
- to make the path before them easier.
- to fill them to overflowing with Your peace and to settle in their spirit the truth about who You are.
- to reveal to them who they are in Christ.
- to help them realize how valuable and precious they are in You. Only You can give everlasting peace, and I plead for that for my children.
- that when my children think of who God is, they remember the abundance of peace You bring.
- to allow them to be led by Your peace and to remember to rely on You.

Thank You that my children have the peace of God.
Thank You that You love my children more than I can imagine.

In Jesus' name I pray, Amen.

Scriptures to Live By

Psalm 29:11
The LORD gives strength to his people;
the LORD blesses his people with peace.

Psalm 42:1
As the deer pants for streams of water,
so my soul pants for you, O God.

Psalm 62:5
Find rest, O my soul, in God alone;
my hope comes from him.

Proverbs 14:30
A heart at peace gives life to the body,
but envy rots the bones.

Matthew 11:28–30
"Come to me, all you who are weary and burdened, and
I will give you rest. Take my yoke upon you and learn
from me, for I am gentle and humble in heart, and you
will find rest for your souls. For my yoke is easy and my
burden is light."

Philippians 4:4–7
Rejoice in the Lord always. I will say it again: Rejoice!
Let your gentleness be evident to all. The Lord is near.
Do not be anxious about anything, but in everything, by
prayer and petition, with thanksgiving, present your
requests to God. And the peace of God, which
transcends all understanding, will guard your
hearts and your minds in Christ Jesus.

Philippians 4:8–9
Finally, brothers, whatever is true, whatever is noble,
whatever is right, whatever is pure, whatever is lovely,

whatever is admirable—if anything is excellent or praiseworthy—think about such things. Whatever you have learned or received or heard from me, or seen in me—put it into practice. And the
God of peace will be with you.

Philippians 4:10–13

I rejoice greatly in the Lord that at last you have renewed your concern for me. Indeed, you have been concerned, but you had no opportunity to show it. I am not saying this because I am in need, for I have learned to be content whatever the circumstances. I know what it is to be in need, and I know what it is to have plenty. I have learned the secret of being content in any and every situation, whether well fed or hungry, whether living in plenty or in want. I can do everything through him who gives me strength.

12

Renew Their Hearts with Joy

> Create in me a pure heart, O God,
> and renew a steadfast spirit within me.
> Do not cast me from your presence
> or take your Holy Spirit from me.
> Restore to me the joy of your salvation
> and grant me a willing spirit to sustain me.
> —Psalm 51:10–12

Steadfast: unwavering; standing your ground; showing resolution; being faithful
Purity: innocence; freedom from guilt
Joy: the emotion of great happiness caused by something exceptionally good or satisfying

In the midst of daily struggles, it is still possible for our children to have joy. It is our wish, isn't it, for our kids to be happy? But for most of us, maintaining joy does not come easily. This is why the Lord teaches us in His Word how to achieve joy, which is accomplished through much prayer.

One important prayer that we should pray regularly is that the Father would renew a right spirit within our children. I have personally seen my child's right spirit transformed through my secretly praying over him. Our children need the joy of the Lord. Let's constantly stay in prayer over their hearts as they grow and learn to seek His presence for themselves.

When Jason was born, he was a precious little bundle of nerves. Even as an infant, he would not lay his head on my shoulder or relax. His hands stayed clinched in a fist and his arms flung wildly. Then when he was three months old, my church had a week-long revival featuring a healing evangelist. God put it on my heart to get Jason from the nursery and take him to the front of the church for prayer. As I stood with him in my arms, the pastor made his way toward me. I was contemplating what to say—"He doesn't relax"—just sounded silly. As the pastor approached, I turned Jason around to face him. Before I could say a word, the pastor touched my head and blew into Jason, while saying, "May the Spirit of God breathe life into this child. Go into him Holy Spirit and touch him." Something instantly changed in my son. He relaxed against my chest for the first time in his life. I believe that God healed something inside of him. From that day on, I knew God had control of Jason's destiny. I knew that God had renewed his spirit.

I learned through this experience how deep the love of God is for us. He longs to renew our spirit and give us joy. We are not guaranteed a completely happy life, but we can sustain a spirit of joy through all circumstances. I've watched this truth personified through my son over the years. He has lived each stage of his life with purpose and direction. On that day nearly twenty-two years ago, God gave Jason the spirit of joy and placed deep into his heart a sense of purpose. I'm so thankful that God was not slow to renew his spirit and fill him with joy of the Lord.

****

It is amazing to me how deep the love of God is for our children. Trust the Lord as you pray over them and expect great things.

Dear heavenly Father,

The challenges my children have faced could steal their joy and cause their spirit to be downcast.
In the name of Jesus, I pray against that

- I come against the spirit of depression, feelings of guilt and condemnation, and pray Your Holy Spirit will replace those negative traits with a right spirit, one that reflects You.
- I ask that You give them a spirit of joy. Continually put a song in their heart and a bounce in their step.
- I ask that You supernaturally cover them with a steadfast spirit that longs to do good.

- I pray, Father, that You would show them Your good works so that they will bless Your name forever.
- I pray that You fill them with a hope, joy, and peace that passes all understanding.

Thank You, Lord, for all the good things You are doing my in children.
Thank You that ___(mention each child by name)___ can see Your good works in her life.
Thank You that my children have Your hope. As long as there is breath in them, I pray they will hope in You.

In Jesus' name I pray, Amen.

Scriptures to Live By

Psalm 51:10
Create in me a pure heart, O God,
and renew a steadfast spirit within me.

Romans 12:2
Do not conform any longer to the pattern of this world,
but be transformed by the renewing of your mind.
Then you will be able to test and approve what God's
will is—his good, pleasing and perfect will.

Romans 15:13
May the God of hope fill you with all joy and peace as
you trust in him, so that you may overflow with hope
by the power of the Holy Spirit.

Colossians 3:12–17
Therefore, as God's chosen people, holy and dearly
loved, clothe yourselves with compassion, kindness,
humility, gentleness and patience. Bear with each other
and forgive whatever grievances you may have against
one another. Forgive as the Lord forgave you. And over
all these virtues put on love, which binds them all
together in perfect unity.

Let the peace of Christ rule in your hearts, since as members of one body you were called to peace. And be thankful. Let the word of Christ dwell in you richly as you teach and admonish one another with all wisdom, and as you sing psalms, hymns and spiritual songs with gratitude in your hearts to God. And whatever you do, whether in word or deed, do it all in the name of the Lord Jesus, giving thanks to God the Father through him.

13

Fill Their Emptiness

> May the God of hope fill you with all joy and peace as
> you trust in him, so that you may overflow with hope
> by the power of the Holy Spirit.
> —Romans 15:13

Emptiness: to be completely spent of emotion
Void: lacking or missing something; a vacancy

I believe that the majority of children who are raised in a single-parent home or have ever lived in a single-parent home have a void in their heart. Although many adjust well and do live a happy life, things are still not exactly as they should be. There is still a longing for that missing relationship. From a young age, children know that something is misplaced, and unfortunately, this world offers many things to those who are seeking to fill a void. Many pre-teens, teenagers, and young adults make decisions solely based on what feels good or fulfilling at the moment, and they grow accustomed to the quick fix. But the results are always sorrow and more emptiness. This is why I believe it is crucial to cover our children in prayer over this specific area. God is eager to restore them and to supernaturally fill their hearts with hope, joy, and peace, allowing them to feel complete and whole.

I have seen many young people search desperately to fill the emptiness that has been left in their heart from a broken relationship with a biological parent. I learned the hard way to recognize the tendency of our hurting children to chase after empty solutions, such as alcohol, drugs, sex, and unhealthy friendships.

Kristin once admitted that she had so much pain from the unstable relationship with her dad that she intentionally made decisions to distract herself from the hurt. Throughout middle school and high school, she had dozens of "boyfriends," thinking that the male attention would fill the emptiness of not having her dad around. (The fact is that out of these dozens, she only actually dated two or three.) In her mind, having a boyfriend provided a security that she did not feel otherwise.

God needs to be—and can be—that security. More than we realize, as parents we need to pray for God's fullness over our children.

****

I plead with all dads to make sure your daughters know how valuable and precious they are to you, and how much you love them. Likewise, I beseech our heavenly Father to cover our girls, especially those without earthly dads, with His love, and to supernaturally fill the void they may be feeling. I plead with all moms of boys to make sure your sons know how much you love them. Even when they're young, find ways to encourage their strength and independence. God created men to need respect, and this can begin in their youth. Raise them to be independent thinkers and confident young men by motivating respect and honor.

How important it is that we pray for Gods supernatural intervention, presence, and protection. We do not always know everything our children are dealing with, but our heavenly Father does.

Dear heavenly Father,

I lift my children before You now and ask that You step into the gap where they have been wounded. My heart longs to make things right for them. Children should not be exposed to the emptiness that comes through the loss of a parent, but they are exposed and thus walk down a path they did not choose. I, therefore, pray in the name of Jesus, that You would

- fill their void.
- turn their emptiness and loneliness into supernatural wholeness. They need You, Lord.
- not only fill that void with Your peace and love, but also seal it with Your Holy Spirit.
- replace emptiness with the spirit of joy.

Thank You for giving them all that they need.
Thank You for filling my children with Your love and a true sense of worthiness.

In Jesus name I pray, Amen.

Scriptures to Live By

Isaiah 58:11
The LORD will guide you always;
he will satisfy your needs in a sun-scorched land
and will strengthen your frame.
You will be like a well-watered garden,
like a spring whose waters never fail.

Psalm 23:5–6
You prepare a table before me
in the presence of my enemies.
You anoint my head with oil;
my cup overflows.
Surely goodness and love will follow me
all the days of my life,
and I will dwell in the house of the LORD
forever.

Matthew 11:28–30
"Come to me, all you who are weary and burdened, and I will give you rest. Take my yoke upon you and learn from me, for I am gentle and humble in heart, and you will find rest for your souls. For my yoke is easy and my burden is light."

Ephesians 3:16–19
I pray that out of his glorious riches he may strengthen you with power through his Spirit in your inner being, so that Christ may dwell in your hearts through faith. And I pray that you, being rooted and established in love, may have power, together with all the saints, to

grasp how wide and long and high and deep is the love of Christ, and to know this love that surpasses knowledge—that you may be filled to the measure of all the fullness of God.

Hebrews 13:5
Keep your lives free from the love of money and be content with what you have, because God has said, "Never will I leave you; never will I forsake you."

14

Take Away Their Feelings of Guilt

> But I lead a blameless life;
> redeem me and be merciful to me.
> —Psalm 26:11

Guilt: a feeling of remorse for some offense, whether real or imagined

Children are emotionally driven during their adolescent years and tend to internalize situations. This could result in blaming themselves for things that are out of their control. Some kids feel at least partially to blame for the breakup of their family, but this is not the case. They generally have no part in the decision to end a marriage; they are, instead, the unfortunate victims. However, we cannot dismiss the fact that they may *feel* responsible. Let's face that reality today, and make sure our children know the truth. We can begin this process by praying over them.

Not only do some children feel a sense of guilt over a divorce, but they may also take on the responsibility for their parents' emotional stability. As you pray over your children, ask the Lord to show you if this is true in your home. Be willing to talk to your child about their feelings and discuss what they may be going through.

Furthermore, our children may have been pulled into the middle of the conflict between two parents they love. Regardless of the safe environment you may have tried to create, children can still take on the responsibility for your happiness. Be mindful of this and watch how your children respond to your sorrow. They love you and may try to prove that love by attempting to fix your sadness, which they are simply not equipped to do.

During Kristin's pre-teen and teenage years, her father often told her how happy he would be if we were still a family. He did this for years—without my knowing anything about these conversations—and all that time she carried the guilt and pain of circumstances that were not at all her fault.

I implore you: Our children need to be reassured that they are not responsible for their parents' decisions. They need to be free to live in an emotionally and spiritually safe environment. Satan, the enemy of God, wants to destroy any hope, peace, and unity within a family. He uses lies to attempt this. Be mindful and pray earnestly.

****

Along with the feelings of guilt that our children carry, they may also feel shame. As you pray over your children, pray that all guilt and shame will be washed away.

Dear heavenly Father,

My children carry a burden, and I thank You now that I can see that. I thank You for the wisdom You have given me to see the needless sense of guilt they have. I pray now in Jesus' name

- that You would remove all feelings of false guilt, shame, or self condemnation. Your Word says that there is no condemnation for those who are in Christ Jesus (Romans 8:1). I thank You for that.
- that You restore ___(mention each child by name)___ heart and mind with a spirit of innocence.
- help my children to have a true reflection of themselves, not carrying the burden or blame for anything out of their control.
- that my children will be able to discern what is actually their responsibility and what is not.
- that if there is any true guilt, something that needs Your forgiveness, ___(mention each child by name)___ would respond to You and be cleansed.
- that starting today my children will begin to see their value and worth in Your eyes.
- if any of my children are ever tempted to believe the lie that they are responsible for my former spouse's actions or mine, remind them that they are not to blame.

- develop a trust in You so that my children can stand boldly in the face of adversity.

Thank You for Your healing touch.
Thank You for loving my child.

In Jesus' name, I pray. Amen.

Scriptures to Live By

Psalm 26:1
Vindicate me, O LORD,
for I have led a blameless life;
I have trusted in the LORD
without wavering.

Ezekiel 18:20
"The soul who sins is the one who will die. The son will not share the guilt of the father, nor will the father share the guilt of the son. The righteousness of the righteous man will be credited to him, and the wickedness of the wicked
will be charged against him."

Romans 8:1
Therefore, there is now no condemnation for those who are in Christ Jesus.

1 Thessalonians 3:13
May he strengthen your hearts so that you will be blameless and holy in the presence of our God and Father when our Lord Jesus comes with all his holy ones.

Hebrews 10:22
Let us draw near to God with a sincere heart in full assurance of faith, having our hearts sprinkled to

cleanse us from a guilty conscience and having our
bodies
washed with pure water.

15

Teach Them to Forgive

> He heals the brokenhearted
> and binds up their wounds.
> He determines the number of the stars
> and calls them each by name.
> Great in our Lord and mighty in power;
> his understanding has no limit.
> —Psalm 147:3–5

Forgive: to stop being angry with someone; to stop blaming; to stop trying to punish

How do we train our children to forgive? I believe the best way is to live it, to be forgivers ourselves. We are the living translation of truth for our children. And regardless of how non-studious they may be in their subjects at school, they are very insightful when it comes to watching how we live and react, which is both fortunate and unfortunate for us. Have you ever reacted harshly toward another driver who pulled out in front of you? What did those reactions teach your child? Everyday moments like these can be opportunities to demonstrate a kind and forgiving heart. It is sometimes difficult, but with God's help, we can be instrumental in training our children in godly living.
This is certainly easier to say than to do. When it comes to people we don't know or interact with regularly, it's a bit easier to forgive, isn't it? The rude driver, for instance. We can convince ourselves that he may be having a hard day, and since we don't know each other it can't be personal. But what about the times when it *is* personal? How do we treat the people in our life who are careless toward our feelings or even purposeful in causing us pain?

There is a very smart tradition I learned from my sister to resolve conflicts within a family. After one person says to another, "I'm sorry," the one offended responds, "I forgive you." I started this a long time ago, and we all still do it to this day. The lesson we have learned through this routine is that it covers much ground for very little sacrifice. Forgiving becomes easier to say and do because it is not foreign to our speech.

We never stop having opportunity to show forgiveness. As long as we have breath, we will have the opportunity to forgive someone at some time. It's part of life, and God will help us, and our children, as we pray for a spirit of forgiveness. Pray that your children will have forgiving hearts, and then allow God to use you as an example.

****

Our children need to be forgivers. When they forgive, they can walk in freedom, but when they do not forgive, they are trapped in bondage and sorrow. Pray intently over your children to have the spirit of forgiveness.

Dear heavenly Father,

I come to You today asking You to help my children learn how to forgive. Your Word clearly explains in Matthew 6:15, that in order for You to forgive us, we must forgive. It is for our own well-being. In Jesus' name, I pray over my children

- that You help them learn to forgive at a young age.
- that You would help them forgive anyone that they feel has done them wrong, including me.
- that they would learn the art of freely forgiving others in a healthy manner.
- that they would let something go rather than holding onto it and letting it grow into bitterness.
- that they would lead lives of true peace and joy.

Thank You for all You have done. Thank You for Your promises and redemption.

In Jesus' name, I pray. Amen.

Scriptures to Live By

Matthew 6:14–15
"For if you forgive men when they sin against you, your heavenly Father
will also forgive you. But if you do not forgive men their sins,
your Father will not forgive your sins."

Matthew 18:21–22
Then Peter came to Jesus and asked, "Lord, how many times shall I
forgive my brother when he sins against me? Up to seven times?"

Jesus answered, "I tell you, not seven times, but seventy-seven times."

Matthew 18:35
"This is how my heavenly Father will treat each of you
unless you forgive your brother from your heart."

Mark 11:25
"And when you stand praying, if you hold anything against anyone, forgive him,
so that your Father in heaven may forgive you your sins."

Luke 6:37
"Do not judge, and you will not be judged. Do not condemn, and you will not be condemned. Forgive, and you will be forgiven."

2 Corinthians 2:7
Now instead, you ought to forgive and comfort him, so that
he will not be overwhelmed by excessive sorrow.

16

Show Them Healthy Boundaries

A righteous man is cautious in friendship,
but the way of the wicked leads them astray.
—Proverbs 12:26

Boundary: a barrier that provides protection

How important it is that our children learn how to put boundaries in place? The culture will attempt to draw them into destructive cycles, feeding them false information about who they are and what they need to become. (If we, as adults are not careful, we too can get caught up in those currents.) And if not covered in prayer, our children are vulnerable. My desire is that you and I learn to pray proactively and diligently. And as we pray, may we also train our children to think for themselves and to install helpful boundaries. They need our instruction and guidance, and they need God's wisdom to know what is good, right, and true.

Friends play an important role in this. In fact, they are a clue to what kind of boundaries our children have set for themselves. They become like the friends they hang with. As a parent, we need to be nosey. As my son would say, "Creep on them." Don't be timid about checking up on their friendships. And if you sense an unhealthy peer, approach wisely, but do approach. Respectfully talk to them about what you are detecting. With teenagers, I have learned that asking questions in a nonthreatening way enables them to feel a little more in control and provides a little safer place to talk. It can also give them an opportunity to make good decisions when they know that we believe they can and will make the right choices. Don't be mistaken; I believe there are times when taking parental authority is necessary for the safety of our child, but we should pray first and ask God for wisdom on how to handle each situation.

When Kristin was in middle school, she developed a good friendship with a sweet girl. Lori (not her real name) was being raised by very strict parents who constantly monitored everything she did. They gave no credit to her good intentions or wise choices. These parents were so fearful of her surroundings that they pulled her out of public school and began homeschooling. They were terrified of all the bad influences that she might succumb to. Instead of praying over her, they were led by fear. And rather than teaching her to withstand peer pressure, make good decisions, and learn from bad ones, they just removed her from the environment.

Although I am a believer in homeschooling, as I myself homeschooled for two years, I do disagree with the theory that you are doing your child a favor by removing peer pressure. Our children must learn how to cope with their peers. The way they learn is to make both good and bad decisions when they have the safety net called *home*. This is where they can best be helped, guided, taught, and trained to suffer consequences. Learning to establish appropriate boundaries at a young age will help them long into adulthood.

Not so long ago I ran into Lori. She shared with me that after high school she moved to another city for college where she made a lot of bad choices. She just wanted to experience life and was tempted by many things during the time of her life when she should have been focused on her future as a young adult. She instead went in a direction that has made her dreams more difficult to achieve.

I encourage you to pray to be Spirit-led while helping your children learn the importance of boundaries. Otherwise, your actions and reactions may tend to be led by fear, resulting in unhealthy decisions, which is not helpful to you or your children.

Dear heavenly Father,

I thank You, Lord, for my children. I pray today

- that You would teach them the importance of healthy boundaries.
- that they would recognize the steps to take in order to establish those boundaries and to be cautious in choosing friends.

- that You would help them to be Spirit led and spiritually aware of their surroundings.
- that You give them wisdom when they're in confusing situations.
- that they can think clearly and make good decisions.
- that they would see the blessed and positive consequence of their boundaries.
- that You would help me to set good examples in this area of life.

Thank You that with You, all things are possible.
Thank You for the ability You have given us to set healthy boundaries.

In Jesus' name, I pray. Amen.

Scriptures to Live By

Deuteronomy 31:6
"Be strong and courageous. Do not be afraid or terrified because of them, for the LORD your God goes with you; he will never leave you nor forsake you."

1 Chronicles 22:13
"Then you will have success if you are careful to observe the decrees and laws
that the LORD gave Moses for Israel. Be strong and courageous.
Do not be afraid or discouraged."

Proverbs 7:21
With persuasive words she led him astray; she seduced him with her smooth talk.

Proverbs 10:17
He who heeds discipline shows the way to life, but whoever ignores correction leads others astray.

Proverbs 12:26
A righteous man is cautious in friendship,
but the way of the wicked leads them astray.

1 John 3:7–8
Dear children, do not let anyone lead you astray. He
who does what is right is righteous, just as he is
righteous. He who does what is sinful is of the devil,
because the devil has been sinning from the beginning.
The reason the Son of God
appeared was to destroy the devil's work.

Psalm 18:2
The LORD is my rock, my fortress and my deliverer;
my God is my rock, in whom I take refuge.
He is my shield and the horn of my salvation, my
stronghold.

17

Help Them Let Go of the Past

> "Forget the former things;
> do not dwell on the past."
> —Isaiah 43:18

Let go: to release and cease dwelling on or worrying about a situation

Properly letting go of our past is vital for our children. It is essential to their growth and maturity. Philippians 3:13–14 reads, "But one thing I do: Forgetting what is behind and straining toward what is ahead, I press on toward the goal to win the prize for which God has called me heavenward in Christ Jesus." In other words, of all the things I do, I forget the past mistakes I have made and I press on to what God has for me.

We must teach this to our children. It will not come naturally, but we are not limited to what comes naturally.

Our minds are powerful, having the ability to both remember and to suppress many events. However, God is in ultimate control. The healing our families need begins by our laying aside those former things, letting go of those things that are haunting us. It is hard to do on our own, but with God's help, our children can completely relinquish past hurts. I am so thankful for that. My children can live life today without dragging along yesterday. They can be free from those burdens.

It wasn't until my daughter was in her twenties and had been married more than a year that she realized how critical it was for her to move on from hurtful memories with her dad. She discovered that although she grieved the missing relationship with him, letting go of what had happened—or had not happened—freed her to live in a healthier relationship with her husband. Certain disappointments and expectations had become a part of her mindset and thus were carried into her marriage. When she made the decision to take the focus off of what could have been and focused on what was, she became liberated. She still loves her dad very much and longs to have a healthy relationship, but she has begun to recognize what is actually healthy for *her*. With God's help she is stronger now and lives with boldness to stand for what is good and right for her and her family.

Letting go of a painful past does not mean that we totally forget our past. It means we do not dwell on painful events and thus allow bitterness to take hold. It means that we can remember the events like we remember a movie, not like a recurring episode of real life that still affects us. But again, we need God's supernatural help.

Press into the heart of God and pray passionately for your children to overcome and let go of any pain from their past. In the presence of God, they will find freedom.

****

As you pray for your children, ask the Lord for supernatural ability to let things go and focus on the good in their lives.

Dear heavenly Father,

You know the things that my children have lived through. Only You truly know what they need to remember and what they need to let go. I ask You in Jesus' name

- to help them let go of those things they have no control over. There are many unfair situations in life that have affected them and many cannot be undone. But I confess that Your grace is sufficient to carry my children.
- for wisdom as my children deal with and let go of their painful past. So many memories have been made. Some of those memories are unpleasant. If my children need to deal with a past experience, please help them. And help me to help them.
- for complete healing of their painful past.
- that when they encounter the bad experiences, my children would learn to walk with You.

Thank You for loving my child more than I can even imagine.
Thank You for keeping my children safe and returning them to me so many times.
Thank You that as You love my children and teach them to surrender all of the junk and emotional scars, You are creating a new heart in each child.

In Jesus' name, I pray. Amen.

Scriptures to Live By

Isaiah 43:18
"Forget the former things;
do not dwell on the past."

Isaiah 65:17
"Behold, I will create
new heavens and a new earth.
The former things will not be remembered,
nor will they come to mind."

Philippians 3:12–14
Not that I have already obtained all this, or have already been made perfect, but I press on to take hold of that for which Christ Jesus took hold of me. Brothers, I do not consider myself yet to have taken hold of it. But one thing I do: Forgetting what is behind and straining toward what is ahead, I press on toward the goal to win the prize for which God has called me heavenward in Christ Jesus.

18

Give Them a Desire to Honor Their Parents

> "Honor your father and your mother, so that you may live long in the land the LORD your God is giving you."
> —Exodus 20:12

Honor: to show respect to others

Most of the decisions we make are based on the honor system. Whether at school or at work, our peers trust us to do the right thing. It's a trust factor. I believe that if our children learn to honor us as parents—as well as any authority God places over them—they will become trustworthy people who walk with integrity.

I found that it was crucial for my children to learn to honor me while they were young, during their grade-school years. I knew that if I could instill an attitude of integrity in them then, all of our lives would be more manageable. I especially needed this as a single parent because I had no one to share lookout duties with. Being able to trust them was crucial. To begin, I focused on the matter of lying. I despise a lying tongue, and the consequences in our family were severe if anyone was caught lying. My children soon learned that life was much easier if they simply told the truth. And the foundation for integrity was established.

My mother was the one who first talked to my son about integrity. When he was a little boy, she would say, "To be a person of integrity you must be honorable, truthful, and trustworthy when no one is looking. You need to be that person so your mom can always trust you and believe you." That helped me realize that I needed to constantly remind my children to be trustworthy. I wanted them to grow up to not only honor me, but to honor the Lord.

Given that our relationships were built around honesty, I have been able to believe my children when they have been wrongly accused. Trust had been so firmly established in our home that if they came to me and gave their word that they were not guilty of some accusation brought against them, I was confident in believing their word. This trust also caused them to stand strong in the face of adversity. They knew that I trusted them, and it gave them courage to do the right thing. With God's help, and through much prayer, I intentionally created a safe place for them to be real. And even when they messed up, my children knew they could tell me and we would work through the issues together. They honored me—and God—by their honesty.

I recall my trust being severely tested when Jason was still in grade school. His best friend at the time had been involved in a crime, and Jason was accused of participating with him. As a result, Jason was required to appear at a state counselor's office for questioning. At some point Jason was made to feel that he might have had something to do with it, so on the way to the counselor's office I asked him firmly, "Jason, did you have anything to do with this?" He replied that he had nothing to do with the incident, and from that moment on, I rested in knowing he had told me the truth. Jason was indeed dismissed and never questioned again, but it was an important lesson for all of us. The counselor told me later that she knew that Jason was being honest because he was forthcoming and bold with all of his answers.

For so many reasons, we must pray that our children learn to lead lives of honor and truthfulness. To this day, both my children place a high value on honesty. We have a mutual respect for one another and I know they honor me. The hours spent in prayer for them has been well worth it.

******

Through prayer and determination, create an environment of trust, honor, and integrity in your home. Ask the Lord to convict your children daily and give them a heart bent toward honoring you as the Scriptures teach.

Dear heavenly Father,

I come to You on behalf of my children, asking You now to bring honor to our relationship. I pray

- that You give __(mention each child by name)__ the desire and ability to honor his parents.
- that by both words and actions my children will obey You by showing honor to their parents.
- that You would help me to be honorable, setting the example for my children.
- that You give her the *desire* to live honorably.
- that my children will feel safe with me and would have the heart to respect me.
- that my children would know how to submit to authority with honor and respect.
- that You would protect my children from the influence of dishonorable people.
- that my children would have the honor to stand up for what is right.

Thank You for hearing my prayer and for wrapping Your arms around my children, causing them to feel safe and to desire to live with honor and integrity.
Thank You that __(mention each child by name)__ honors me, even when she/he may not understand or agree with my decisions.
Thank You that even today my children will begin to honor me through their words and actions.

In Jesus' name, I pray. Amen.

Scriptures to Live By

Romans 2:10
Glory, honor and peace for everyone who does good:
first for the Jew, then for the Gentile.

Romans 12:10
Be devoted to one another in brotherly love.
Honor one another above yourselves.

Ephesians 6:2
"Honor your father and mother"—which is the
first commandment with a promise.

Hebrews 13:18
Pray for us. We are sure that we have a clear conscience
and desire to live honorably in every way.

19

Teach Them Humility

> Humble yourselves before the Lord,
> and he will lift you up.
> —James 4:10

Humble: not thinking too highly of oneself, putting others first

A person who is truly humble has a servant's heart. We live in a selfish world where we are prodded to do whatever it takes to get to the top. However, God's principles are stationed on humility. That is, we are to put others before ourselves. What would happen if we were to teach the next generation the art of humility? I challenge you to begin looking for teachable moments to show your children how to serve others. In doing so, you will plant seeds of humility and compassion.

One year during Christmas break I took my children to New Mexico for a ski vacation. I hadn't much money, so we saved for months before our trip. I budgeted very carefully, even arranging to stay at a resort that was just one day's drive away. I paid cash for everything, and each day had its designated amount.

Each morning we drove through the city on our way to the ski lift area, and each morning we would pass a homeless man sitting on a corner. The same homeless man every day. Although I worked really long hours to afford the luxury of a vacation, and frankly wondered why he couldn't find a job and work also, my heart hurt for him. I couldn't help but feel sad over his predicament. I imagined a whole string of circumstances that might have caused his homelessness.

One morning the kids and I talked about that man. They wondered why he would sit there and how a person becomes homeless. I reminded them how blessed we were to be on a vacation and have a home in Texas with a warm bed at night and food to eat. Then as the road took us up the mountain and we would see the ski lifts, we would soon forget the homeless man. One particular morning before heading through town, we stopped at a grocery store to pick up our lunch and snacks for the day. I also bought a box of cereal for our remaining breakfasts.

Heading through town, I turned the corner in the direction of the mountain, and there he was—the same man, sitting alone. And then God spoke to my heart. *Give him the box of cereal.* My first reaction was confusion because I know that cereal is really not all that nutritious. But I knew instantly that this was not really about the man on the corner, but about the people in my car. I pulled over and said, "Jason, run back and give that man this box of cereal. He's probably really hungry and needs it more than we do." For a second he stared at me blankly, but then grabbed the box. He ran back to the man, and gave him the cereal. When he returned to the car, I asked, "Did he say anything to you?" Jason replied, "Just 'thank you.' But, Mom, what about the milk?" The kids still remember the homeless man on the corner who got a box of cereal—without milk.

What we do as parents greatly impacts our children's wills, minds, and emotions. They do what we do, not what we say we should do. My children are givers. Did that one act of feeding cereal to a homeless man change them in an instant? Probably not, but I wonder if it did indeed plant seeds of God's truth. Life is not all about us. And when we accept that, there begins the spirit of humility.

Not long ago, Jason gave a homeless man his brand new shoes right off his feet. He walked away barefooted for the love of Christ. Many times Kristin has seen the need of a single mother and has stepped up to meet it. She'll often rally others who can help by pooling resources.

Serving others is humbling, and it helps break down the wall of our pride. And with pride removed, God can move and do great things in us and through us.

As you pray over your children for humility, be ready and willing to humble yourself as well. Pray that your children willingly choose humility, so that the Lord will fill them with His grace and power.

Dear heavenly Father,

Thank You that You are giving my children the heart to serve You. I may not see evidence of this yet, but I know You are working in them. I pray now in the name of Jesus that

- You would open up their hearts to humility.
- You would show my children how to lay pride aside and consider the good of others before themselves.
- my children would have an eternal perspective of life.
- my children would understand that life is bigger than their own private world.
- You would open doors of service opportunities for my children where they can experience You working through them.
- You would rid my children of vanity.
- my children would freely give love and grace to others, always seeking to put others first.
- my children would always know their need for You.

Thank You for the love and grace You have shown us.
Thank You for never giving up on my children, and for continuing to draw them to You.
Thank You for the humble example of Your son.

In Jesus' name I pray, Amen.

Scriptures to Live By

Ephesians 4:2
Be completely humble and gentle; be patient,
bearing with one another in love.

James 4:6
But he gives us more grace. That is why Scripture says:
"God opposes the proud but gives grace to the
humble."

1 Peter 3:8
Finally, all of you, live in harmony with one another; be sympathetic,
love as brothers, be compassionate and humble.

1 Peter 5:5
Young men, in the same way be submissive to those who are older. All of you, clothe yourselves with humility toward one another, because, "God opposes the proud but gives grace to the humble."

1 Peter 5:6
Humble yourselves, therefore, under God's mighty hand,
that he may lift you up in due time.

Luke 18:14
"I tell you that this man, rather than the other, went home justified before God. For everyone who exalts himself will be humbled, and he who humbles himself will be exalted."

Psalm 147:6
The LORD sustains the humble
but casts the wicked to the ground.

20

Show Them Your Plan

> "For I know the plans I have for you," declares the
> LORD, "plans to prosper
> you and not to harm you, plans to give you hope and a
> future."
> —Jeremiah 29:11

Show: to reveal; to make known

There are so many influences pulling at our children. I wished many times that I could have kept my children in a bubble, safe from all the harm and danger in the world. However, that was not an option. But what was—and is—an option is the power of prayer. We parents can be a real and powerful force in the lives of our children by simply praying over them every day. Does this guarantee a life free from hurt, pain, or bad decisions? No. There is an enemy that seeks to destroy each one of us, but the Word of God is more powerful than anything we will face. And I can testify that our heavenly Father will never leave us. I have seen the presence of God many times as my children have been hurt or badly influenced by others, and God stepped in to heal, protect, and transform them. To this day I am amazed by all that God has done for my family.

As I mentioned before, Kristin was strong-willed. She loved to prove her independence in most everything she did. She told me many times that she *wanted* to learn things by her own mistakes rather than listening to my counsel. We struggled for many years. The problem for me was that she was very charming and could avoid trouble with teachers, peers, and friends—all of which gave her a false sense of invincibility. But I kept praying. I knew God was after her heart, and I knew it was a matter of time.

During her first year at college, Kristin's life took a turn. When she called one evening, I knew something was wrong. She was crying and told me to sit down. She had been dating a man from work and had gotten pregnant. I remember being oddly calm, and the Lord spoke to my heart, "I'm getting her attention, and it could be much worse." God is so merciful on us, isn't He? Although I was initially sad for the timing and circumstances, I had spent so much time in prayer over my daughter that I knew God had a bigger agenda in mind. I had learned to trust Him with these things.

Children live with little thought about tomorrow. They are deceived into thinking that there will be no serious consequences for what they do. But God wants so much more for them. He has an amazing plan for our children's lives (Jeremiah 29:11).

God used that sweet baby to change the direction of my daughter's life. It was an act of God's mercy and love. Kristin received that change with great grace and maturity, and she has become an amazing woman and mom who uses her testimony for God's glory.

****

Pray that God begins to open your children's minds to show them a greater plan and vision for their lives. As that unfolds, you must trust the Lord. He knows exactly what your children need and who He created them to be.

Dear heavenly Father,

I pray that by Your Spirit You would draw my children close and reveal to them their personal destiny and purpose. I pray

- that they would learn to recognize and listen to Your still small voice.
- that as they hear You, they will follow You.
- that You would grant them Your power and wisdom.
- that my children will lean on You for help, and when challenged will draw strength from Your Spirit.
- that when they stray or makes mistakes, You will bring them back on track.
- that as they are tested, You will empower them to overcome those challenges and be successful.

- and I pray in the name of Jesus against the powers of darkness that want my children to fail.

Thank You that You will never leave them nor forsake them.
Thank You that You have a good plan for my children.
Thank You that my children can trust Your Word.
Thank You that You will help them every step of the way.
Thank You that I can trust You with my child.
Thank You that nothing can touch my child without Your permission.

In Jesus' name I pray, Amen.

Scriptures to Live By

Proverbs 16:3
Commit to the LORD whatever you do,
and your plans will succeed.

Proverbs 16:9
In his heart a man plans his course,
but the LORD determines his steps.

Jeremiah 29:11
"For I know the plans I have for you," declares the
LORD, "plans to prosper you and not to harm you,
plans to give you hope and a future."

Jeremiah 31:3
The LORD appeared to us in the past, saying: "I have
loved you with an everlasting love; I have drawn you
with loving-kindness."

John 6:44
"No one can come to me unless the Father who sent
me draws him,
and I will raise him up at the last day."

Hebrews 10:22
Let us draw near to God with a sincere heart in full assurance of faith,
having our hearts sprinkled to cleanse us from a guilty conscience
and having our bodies washed with pure water.

James 4:7–9
Submit yourselves, then, to God. Resist the devil, and he will flee from you.
Come near to God and he will come near to you.

Conclusion

Thank you for taking the time to pray and to submit under the loving hand of our Father. He has begun a great work in you and in your children. Be encouraged to continue to turn to the Lord with all of your life, your treasures, your desires, your dreams, your hurts, your fears, your burdens, and all that is within you. He forever longs to radically change you and your children from the inside out.

As we conclude, always remember that the Lord is your refuge. The seasons of life may change as your children grow and experience new things, so use this book as a tool to help you through each stage. It is my prayer that through this time of reading and praying over yourself and over your children, that you have developed the great habit of running to Him.

Your children will thank you for pursuing God, and the generations to come will be blessed by your heart of obedience. First Samuel 12:23 reads, "As for me, far be it from me that I should sin against the LORD by failing to pray for you. And I will teach you the way that is good and right." May the Lord bless you and shine on you as you follow His ways.

Made in the USA
Charleston, SC
19 February 2017